Kids' Power Too:
Words
To
Grow
By

Cathey Brown
Betty D'Angelo-LaPorte
Jerry Moe

ISBN 0-9653789-0-X

Published by: ImaginWorks
4300 McArthur Avenu
Dallas, Texas 75209

Table of Contents

Dedication

We lovingly dedicate this book to our families.

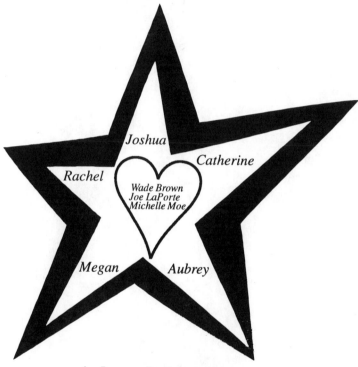

Acknowledgments

Special thanks to the following people who helped make this book a reality.

Kirsteen Anderson

Connie Brown

Karen Chatfield

David Fischer

Peter Ways

David Weaver

Jeff Wright

Introduction

Welcome to *Kids' Power, Too: Words to Grow By*. This is a book written just for you. It has an affirmation for you to read and think about for each day of the year. Affirmations are positive statements that can help you to think, feel, and act in healthy ways. Affirmations can guide you in living each day.

Growing up today can be a challenge. Many children live in families that are dealing with problems and difficulties. Often children think these family problems are all their fault. You'll learn in this book that they are not. You learn and study to become "head smart." This book will also help you become "heart smart."

Kids' Power, Too can help you feel better about yourself. It may help you to learn new skills and ways to grow up healthy and strong. You may use this book at school, church or synagogue, in a special group, or at home with a caring parent or other adult. You will come to realize how very special you truly are.

This book is for you. If you have your own copy, you might want to read it all by yourself sometimes. You have the right to do this. Let your parent or other adult know this is what you'd like to do. Feel free to write, draw, or color in your book. You may want to write down your thoughts or copy the daily affirmation in your own handwriting. Find a safe place for your book so you can use it every day. Find someone you trust to discuss thoughts or feelings you might have while reading it. This sharing activity can be very helpful.

May this book help you to grow and develop new skills. May it lead you to health and happiness. Most of all, it may help you in always remembering you are one-of-a-kind, special, beautiful, and precious.

Safe People

Throughout this book, you'll see the words **safe people.** What does that mean? Safe people are individuals who care about you. They take the time to listen to your thoughts and feelings. They can be very helpful. They don't hurt you. Safe people have many special qualities:

1. *They listen to you.*
2. *They enjoy spending time with you.*
3. *They care about you.*
4. *They offer helpful suggestions and support.*
5. *They are trustworthy. You can count on them and feel comfortable with them.*

Many people in your life could be safe people. A parent, grandparent, other relative, neighbor, or teacher could be a safe person. So could a counselor, coach, minister or rabbi, police officer, or a friend's parent. Lots of different people can possess these many qualities. Think about who can be the safe people in your life. Safe people are friends who can help you.

Safe Places

Throughout this book, you'll also see the words **safe places.** What does that mean? Safe places are spaces where you are out of the way of harm. You can't be hurt there. You are free to think, feel, dream, play, and even cry there. In a safe place you can just be yourself. We all need safe places.

Many places could be safe for you. Your house, the playground, school, your room, a safe person's office, and a friend's house could be safe places. It's helpful to have many safe places where you are free to think, feel, and be yourself. Think about what places might be safe for you. Safe places can protect you.

God

Throughout this book you'll see the word **God.** People have many different names for God, and beliefs about god. You have the right to have your own beliefs and understanding of who or what God is. You might even have your own name for God. God created the mountains, the stars, the oceans, and all living things. God created you and me as well. As a child of God, you are full of beauty and goodness. You are blessed with special gifts and talents that are yours alone. God made you one-of-a-kind.

God is a special friend who loves and cares about each of us. We can talk to God about our problems, thoughts, feelings, mistakes, and successes. God always listens and is there for us. We are never alone, because God is watching over all of us.

 am

a very

special kid.

JANUARY
1

My
feelings
are okay.

JANUARY
2

I

will laugh
and play
with
my friends.

JANUARY
3

I am
important.
I deserve to
be safe.

**JANUARY
4**

I can
learn how
to handle
my problems.

**JANUARY
5**

It's
okay
to
be a kid.

JANUARY
6

All my

choices

have

consequences.

JANUARY
7

I have
the right
to be myself.

JANUARY

8

Today
I will take
care of
me.

JANUARY
9

can

believe in

many things.

**JANUARY
10**

 I am

growing

and changing

every day.

JANUARY
11

I

can show

my feelings.

JANUARY
12

friend is very special. I can make friends.

JANUARY 13

deserve

to be

safe today.

JANUARY
14

It's
okay to ask
for help.
I'm worth it.

JANUARY
15

Kids

come in all

SHAPES, sizes,

and colors. Hooray!

JANUARY
16

I can
choose what's
best
for me.

JANUARY
17

I have
the right
to my feelings.

JANUARY
18

I will
take time
to rest
and relax.

JANUARY
19

I am

a child of God

full of goodness.

JANUARY
20

I like
myself just
the way I am.

**JANUARY
21**

I can

tell my feelings

without hurting

myself or others.

JANUARY
22

I can
ask safe family
members for
love and help.

JANUARY
23

Safe
people don't
make fun
of my tears.

JANUARY
24

I will

take care

of myself if

people yell

and fight.

JANUARY

25

can smile,

giggle, laugh,

and grin.

JANUARY 26

I

can choose
to think just
about today.

I have

the right

to ask for help.

JANUARY
28

Today
I can have
fun
and play.

od

has blessed me.

I am very special.

**JANUARY
30**

 am

special, I am me.

There's no one

I would rather be.

JANUARY
31

It's okay
to cry when I'm
sad, hurt, or lonely.

**FEBRUARY
1**

There are
people who
love me. I am
not alone.

**FEBRUARY
2**

When
my world
is scary I can
find safe places.

FEBRUARY
3

I can
ask for help
when I have
a problem.

FEBRUARY
4

I can
have fun
by using
my imagination.

FEBRUARY
5

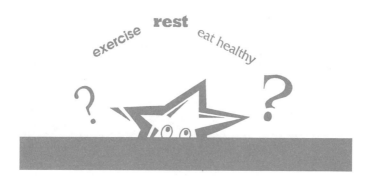

exercise **rest** eat healthy

I
can choose
to take good
care of my body.

FEBRUARY

6

I have
the right to
feel my feelings.

FEBRUARY
7

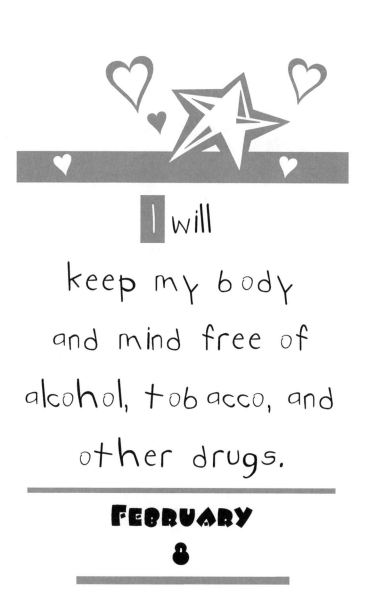

I will

keep my body
and mind free of
alcohol, tobacco, and
other drugs.

FEBRUARY

8

od

loves me,

even when I make

a mistake.

FEBRUARY
9

I am

a child of

God with many

special talents.

FEBRUARY
10

I

can have more
than one feeling
at a time.

**FEBRUARY
11**

care about
myself. I care
about other people.

FEBRUARY
12

I
am special --
it's important
for me to
be safe.

**FEBRUARY
13**

The

problems

in my family

are not my fault.

FEBRUARY
14

 can

see my

great smile

in the mirror.

FEBRUARY
15

can make

good decisions

if I think carefully.

**FEBRUARY
16**

I have
the right
to be a kid.

**FEBRUARY
17**

I can
choose to give
hugs. I can ask
safe people for hugs.

FEBRUARY
18

I believe
in God.
I believe in me.

**FEBRUARY
19**

Today
I will
feel good
about myself.

FEBRUARY
20

My
feelings
belong to me.

FEBRUARY
21

I can
deal with
family problems.

FEBRUARY
22

I

can make

safe choices

today.

FEBRUARY
23

If
my parents
drink alcohol or use
other drugs,
it's not my fault.

**FEBRUARY
24**

I can
have fun
today. I will
laugh and play.

**FEBRUARY
25**

can choose
to take good
care of my mind.

**FEBRUARY
26**

I have
the right
to make mistakes.

FEBRUARY
27

I am
important.
Today I will take
care of myself.

FEBRUARY 28

I can

celebrate

this

special day.

**FEBRUARY
29**

When
I feel sad
and lonely, I can
ask God for help.

MARCH
1

God

smiled

the day

I was born.

**MARCH
2**

My
feelings
guide me
through the day.

MARCH
3

I have safe people in my life. Family members and friends can be safe people.

MARCH
4

Safe
People are
people who care,
people I can trust.

MARCH
5

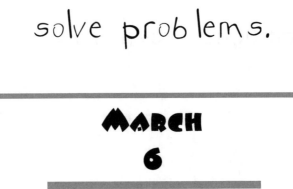

I can
learn new
ways to
solve problems.

**MARCH
6**

I

am

a

kid.

MARCH
7

Today
I can choose
to stay
safe and healthy.

MARCH
8

I have
the right
to be a kid.

MARCH
9

I can
take time to
be quiet and
listen to
my heart.

MARCH 10

I believe
God
loves me.

MARCH
11

Today

I will celebrate

the good in me.

MARCH
12

I have
many different
feelings. All my
feelings are okay.

MARCH
13

I
can find

good in

others.

MARCH
14

There are
safe people
who can
help me.

MARCH
15

I am
capable
of solving
my problems.

**MARCH
16**

 have
friends.
Today I'll ask
a friend to play.

**MARCH
17**

I

can learn
from the
choices I make.

MARCH
18

 have
the right
to be myself.

MARCH
19

Today
I'll do one
special thing
just for me.

MARCH
20

I am
God's
creation.

MARCH
21

I am
one of
a kind.

MARCH
22

I

believe love

is a

special feeling.

 have a

special friend.

It's me!

MARCH
24

I
can find
safe people
in my life.

MARCH
25

The
problems in
my family aren't
caused by me.

**MARCH
26**

My job
is to
be a kid.

**MARCH
27**

NO!

It's
okay to
say "no" to
my friends.

MARCH
28

I have
the right
to be heard.

MARCH
29

I'll take care of myself today by telling my feelings to someone I trust.

MARCH
30

Today I will talk to God about my feelings and thoughts.

**MARCH
31**

Today I will
celebrate
who I am.

APRIL
1

 can make
choices about
sharing my feelings.

**APRIL
2**

I
will hug
someone
I love today.

APRIL
3

can be

myself

in safe places.

**APRIL
4**

I am
learning how
to get help
when I have
a problem.

APRIL
5

Today
I will take
time to
play a game.

**APRIL
6**

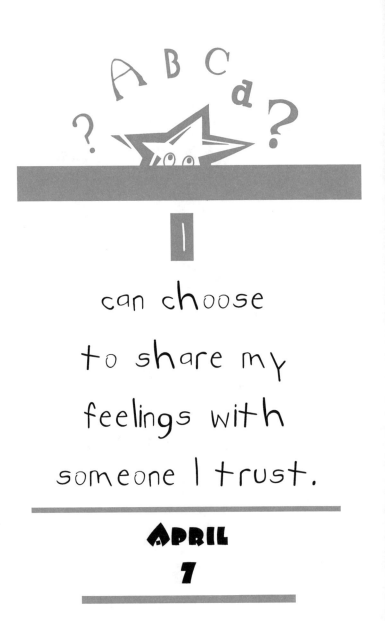

I

can choose
to share my
feelings with
someone I trust.

APRIL
7

 have
the right
to get help.

APRIL
8

I am
my own
best friend
when I am
good to myself.

**APRIL
9**

 can

treat myself
and others with
respect. We are all
God's children.

**APRIL
10**

I will

do good things

for me.

APRIL
11

 am
capable of dealing
with my feelings.
I can ask for help.

**APRIL
12**

1

will laugh with
my friends --
not at them.

**APRIL
13**

can find
grown-ups
who will listen
to me.

**APRIL
14**

If my
parents fight,
it is not
my fault.

APRIL
15

Today
I celebrate
being
a kid.

APRIL
16

I
will do
kid stuff
today.

APRIL
17

I have
the right to
show my feelings.

APRIL
18

I will

learn about

healthy foods

and make

healthy choices.

APRIL
19

I have
a very special
friend who loves
me: God.

APRIL
20

I am
special on
the inside and
on the outside.

APRIL
21

I am
learning to share
my feelings.

**APRIL
22**

It's
okay to
take care
of myself first.

APRIL
23

The next
time I have
a problem,
I will talk to
a safe person.

**APRIL
24**

Today
I can learn
from the
mistakes I make.

**APRIL
25**

Today
I will use my
imagination.
I will have fun.

**APRIL
26**

can choose
many ways to
take care
of myself.

**APRIL
27**

I have
the right
to talk about
my feelings.

APRIL
28

Today
I will take care
of my mind
by reading.

APRIL
29

God
is part
of my life.

APRIL
30

I believe
in me.
I really do.

MAY
1

Today
I will share
my feelings with
someone I trust.

MAY
2

I

am a part
of God's family.
I am not alone.

 MAY
 3

oday
I will make
safe choices.

4

 can
ask for help
when I have
a problem.

**MAY
5**

Today
I will do
fun
kid things.

MAY
6

I

will do
something
today that's
just for me.

MAY
7

I have
the right
to talk about
my problems.

MAY

8

I can
forgive myself
when I make
a mistake.

MAY
9

God

cares

about me.

I can

be the

best I can be.

MAY
11

I

can find friends
to talk to about
my feelings.

I

am learning
how to be
a friend.

**MAY
13**

oday
I will spend
time with
safe people.

MAY
14

 have
the skills
to help me
solve problems.

**MAY
15**

I can

draw pictures

and sing

some songs.

MAY
16

I

can

think

for myself.

I have
the right to
my thoughts
and feelings.

MAY
18

I will
find time
to do something
I enjoy.

MAY
19

oday I
celebrate that
God loves me.

MAY
20

I am
special and
I have
special talents.

MAY
21

can't change
how other
people feel or act.

MAY
22

Safe
family members
can be my friends.

MAY
23

can learn
ways to take
care of myself
and be safe.

**MAY
24**

I can
ask for help
when things
are tough.

 Helping

my friends

can be fun.

MAY
26

I

can learn
from all the
different choices
I make.

MAY
27

have
the right
to say "no."

MAY
28

It's
okay to
ask for help.
I'm worth it.

MAY
29

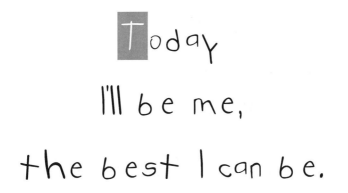

Today
I'll be me,
the best I can be.

MAY
30

I am

blessed with

many talents.

MAY
31

1

can talk to

safe people

about my feelings.

JUNE
1

When my
family has
problems,
I can take good
care of myself.

**JUNE
2**

I

am learning

about

safe places.

JUNE
3

I can
forgive myself
when I
mess up.

JUNE
4

I will
celebrate
me for
being myself.

JUNE
5

Today
I have
a choice
about my feelings.

JUNE
6

I have
the right
to enjoy myself.

JUNE
7

I can
learn
something new
every day.

JUNE
8

When I'm worried or scared, I can talk to God.

JUNE
9

I can

be happy

about a lot of

things in my life.

JUNE
10

When I
feel happy
I can share it
with others.

JUNE
11

I

believe that
God is a part
of my family.

Safe
people
listen
to me.

JUNE
13

I will
take care
of me by
solving a problem.

JUNE
14

I have friends.
Today, I'll spend
time with
one of them.

JUNE
15

I

can choose
to forgive people
when they make
a mistake.

JUNE
16

I have
the right
to make choices
that are good
for me.

JUNE
17

1

deserve to
be good
to myself.

I believe
this day
is a gift
from God.

**JUNE
19**

Yea

me!

JUNE
20

I can

show my angry
feelings in ways
that don't hurt
myself or others.

JUNE
21

Today
I will be a
friend to
myself.

JUNE
22

I

am special.
It is important
for me
to stay safe.

JUNE
23

I can
have patience.
Hard times
don't last forever.

JUNE
24

I can laugh, even if things don't go my way.

JUNE 25

I

will think
about the
consequences
of my choices.

JUNE
26

I have
the right
to be safe.

JUNE
27

Today
I will take
good care
of my body
by etercising.

JUNE
28

Lots of friends care about me. God is one of them.

JUNE
29

There is

no one else

exactly like me.

JUNE
30

If I
feel sad today,
I will talk to
someone I trust.

**JULY
1**

I
will look
for the good
in others today.

_____

**JULY
2**

_____

I

can find
adults who help
me solve problems.

JULY
3

I can

be free

to be me.

Let's celebrate!

**JULY
4**

With
help I can
cope with
family problems.

JULY
5

can make

good choices

with the help

of safe people.

JULY
6

I have
the right to
be listened to.

JULY
7

Today
I can have
fun by
singing silly songs.

JULY
8

I am
a child
of God --
full of love.

JULY
9

I believe
I am lovable
and capable.

**JULY
10**

When I
feel angry,
I can pound a
pillow or scribble
a picture.

JULY
11

I

can be

a friend

to myself.

**JULY
12**

Today
I will remember
there are
safe people
in my life.

JULY
13

Everyone
has problems.
Some are mine,
some aren't.

**JULY
14**

Kids

come in all

shapes, SIZES,

and colors. Terrific!

JULY
15

Today
I can choose
to play a game
or just to relax.

JULY
16

I have
the right
to be myself.

JULY
17

I will
share my
plans with
someone I trust.

JULY
18

I will

live God's love

by treating myself

and others well.

**JULY
19**

Today
I like myself
just the way
I am.

JULY
20

It's okay
to feel scared
the first time
I do something.

JULY
21

I can
only change
myself -- I can't
change others.

JULY
22

If
scary things
happen I can
find ways
to be safe.

**JULY
23**

Fixing
other people's
problems is
not my job.

JULY
24

Today
I will explore
and
be curious.

**JULY
25**

I can think
about my choices
when I have
a problem.

JULY
26

I have

the right

to make choices

that are good

for me.

**JULY
27**

Today
I will eat foods
that are
good for me.

JULY
28

Rainbows

are one of the

gifts

from God.

**JULY
29**

Today
I'll use my
talents to
help myself.

**JULY
30**

It's okay
to feel angry or hurt
if someone
breaks a promise.

JULY
31

I

can show
love by being
kind to someone.

Safe people
don't make
fun of me
when I cry.

AUGUST
2

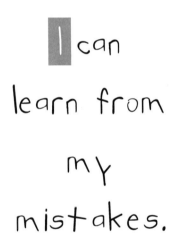

I can
learn from
my
mistakes.

AUGUST
3

I can
enjoy learning
to do
new things.

AUGUST
4

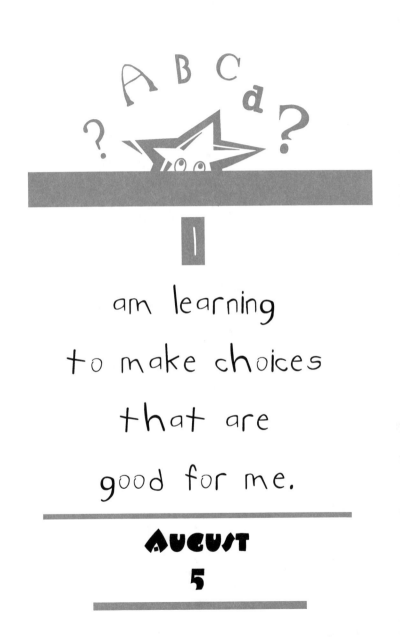

I
am learning
to make choices
that are
good for me.

AUGUST
5

I have
the right
to take good
care of myself.

I am
celebrating me
when I am good
to myself.

7

 can

feel God's

love today. I

believe there is hope.

AUGUST
8

I am
terrific.
I am a miracle.

9

My

feelings are

an important

part of me.

AUGUST
10

Today
I can be a
good friend
by sharing.

AUGUST
11

There are
safe people and
safe places to
help me.
I can ask for help.

**AUGUST
12**

I can
ask for help
when I
get confused.

AUGUST
13

 I will
play and
be a
kid today.

AUGUST
14

 will take
my time
when making
choices.

AUGUST
15

I have
the right
to make choices.

AUGUST
16

 am
learning that
some rules can help
keep me safe.

**AUGUST
17**

 believe

God is looking

out for me today.

AUGUST
18

I believe
in my talents.
I believe in me.

AUGUST
19

It is
okay to cry,
when I am
sad or happy.

AUGUST
20

Today
I can
make new
friends.

AUGUST
21

 deserve

to be treated

with respect.

 am
capable of
solving
problems.

**AUGUST
23**

 am
growing and
changing
every day.

? A B C d ?

Today
I will make
choices that
are good for me.

AUGUST
25

 have
the right
to choose what
is best for me.

**AUGUST
26**

Today
I will take
time to do
what I enjoy.

**AUGUST
27**

Today

I can use the

talents God has

given me.

AUGUST
28

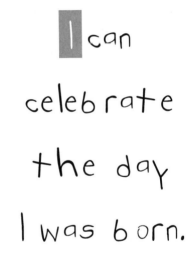

I can
celebrate
the day
I was born.

AUGUST
29

I

believe my
feelings
are okay.

AUGUST
30

There
are people
who love me.
I am not alone.

AUGUST
31

can make

safe choices

today.

**SEPTEMBER
1**

It's okay
to ask for
help if I can't
do something
by myself.

**SEPTEMBER
2**

I can
run, laugh and
play. I will be
a kid today.

SEPTEMBER
3

Today
I will choose
to take good
care of myself.

SEPTEMBER
4

I have
the right
to talk about
my feelings.

SEPTEMBER
5

I will

take time

to be quiet and

think my own

thoughts.

SEPTEMBER

6

oday
I can pray
to God.
There is hope.

**SEPTEMBER
7**

Celebrate!
I am a
child of God.

can have

a lot of

different feelings.

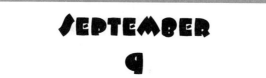

am my
own special
friend.

believe
it's important
for me
to be safe.

SEPTEMBER 11

If my
parents separate
or divorce,
it's not my fault.

___

I can

choose

to be a

kid today.

SEPTEMBER
13

 am capable
of making
good choices.

I have
the right
to talk about
my problems.

SEPTEMBER
15

Today
I will take
good care of myself
by listening
to music.

SEPTEMBER
16

I can

trust God.

God cares about

what I'm doing.

SEPTEMBER
17

Everyone has
special qualities.
Today I will
celebrate mine.

SEPTEMBER
18

When
I feel afraid,
adults I trust
can help me.

enjoy
being with
my friends.

I
will talk
to a safe person
when I have
a problem.

SEPTEMBER
21

I can
learn new
ways to cope
with problems.

SEPTEMBER
22

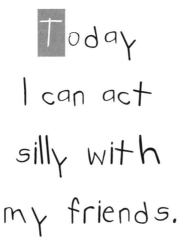

Today
I can act
silly with
my friends.

SEPTEMBER
23

I

can choose

to trust

God today.

SEPTEMBER
24

I have
the right
to feel scared
and say I am afraid.

SEPTEMBER
25

I will
be good
to myself.
I will get
enough sleep.

SEPTEMBER
26

I can

talk to God

anytime and

anyplace.

**SEPTEMBER
27**

I am

special in

many ways.

**SEPTEMBER
28**

have friends
I can talk to
about my feelings.

SEPTEMBER
29

---

am learning

to be

a friend

to others.

SEPTEMBER 30

Safe people
let
me talk.

OCTOBER
1

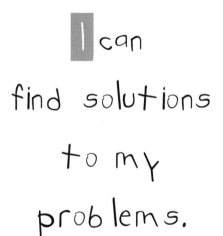

I can
find solutions
to my
problems.

OCTOBER
2

I am
creative
when I color
or paint.

OCTOBER
3

Asking
for help
can be a
good choice.

**OCTOBER
4**

 have
the right
to change
my mind.

OCTOBER
5

Today
I will
thank God
for loving me.

OCTOBER
6

I can

celebrate my

friendship with God

through music.

**OCTOBER
7**

I can

do good

things

for myself.

I can
share my
feelings without
hurting myself
or others.

OCTOBER
9

I

will seek

out

friends today.

OCTOBER
10

It is
important for
me to
be safe.

OCTOBER
11

I am
responsible
for the way
I act, not the
way others act.

OCTOBER
12

I feel
good inside
when I
play fair.

**OCTOBER
13**

TODAY

can enjoy
today and
not worry
about tomorrow.

OCTOBER
14

I have
the right
to my tears.

OCTOBER
15

Today
I'll be kind
to
myself.

**OCTOBER
16**

Both
sunshine and
clouds are gifts
from God.

**OCTOBER
17**

I am
the best
at being me.

OCTOBER
18

I can't change
how others
act or feel.
I can change me.

OCTOBER
19

Safe
people
can be part
of my family.

OCTOBER 20

There
are people
who can
understand and
help me.

OCTOBER 21

My many
strengths
help me to
solve problems.

OCTOBER
22

Today
I will give
a smile
to a friend.

OCTOBER
23

 can make

a safe choice

today.

OCTOBER
24

 have
the right to
think good thoughts
about myself.

**OCTOBER
25**

Today
I'll do one
special thing
just for me.

**OCTOBER
26**

I am a part
of a family,
school, and community.
I am a part of
the human race.

**OCTOBER
27**

I can

do the

best

I can do.

OCTOBER
28

When
I feel lonely,
adults I trust
can help me.

OCTOBER 29

can be

a special

friend.

_____

**OCTOBER
30**

_____

It's
important
for me
to be safe.

**OCTOBER
31**

 can
have patience.
Tough times
don't last forever.

**NOVEMBER
1**

I will
play
with a
toy today.

**NOVEMBER
2**

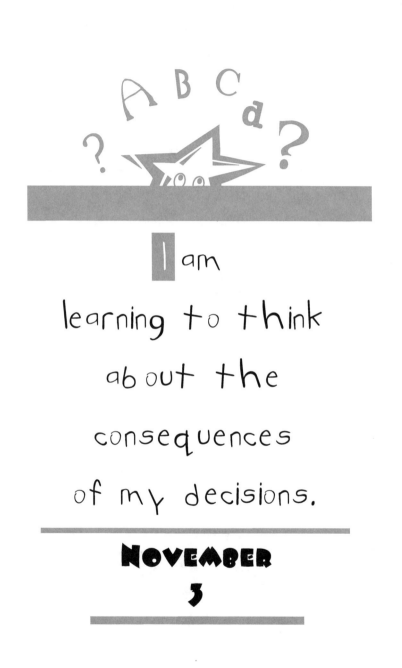

I am

learning to think

about the

consequences

of my decisions.

NOVEMBER
3

I have
the right
to say "no"
to things that
can hurt me.

NOVEMBER
4

I will keep my body and mind free of alcohol, tobacco, and other drugs.

NOVEMBER
5

I believe
God is love.
God loves me.

NOVEMBER
6

Today
I will look
for the good
in me.

NOVEMBER
7

I

can rest

when I feel

tired.

NOVEMBER
8

There
are people
who care
about me.
I am not alone.

NOVEMBER
9

Safe people
keep
their word.

NOVEMBER
10

Families
can get help
in solving
problems.

NOVEMBER
11

Today
I can giggle
at
funny things.

NOVEMBER
12

can enjoy
today and not
worry about
yesterday.

**NOVEMBER
13**

 have
the right to
my own space.

**NOVEMBER
14**

Today
I will
be easy
on myself.

**NOVEMBER
15**

Today I will
show God's love
by treating myself
and others well.

NOVEMBER
16

Today
I will find
the good in me.

**NOVEMBER
17**

Y
feelings
guide me
through the day.

**NOVEMBER
18**

I will ask
safe family members
for help & love
during the holidays.

NOVEMBER 19

I will find
safe people & places
to help me
during the holidays.

NOVEMBER
20

I can
turn to others
for help
during the holidays.

NOVEMBER
21

Today
I can think
about my
hopes and dreams.

NOVEMBER
22

can choose
to make a
new start today.

NOVEMBER
23

I have
the right to
say "no" to
alcohol, tobacco,
and other drugs.

NOVEMBER 24

Today
I am
thankful
for being me.

**NOVEMBER
25**

I believe

in God, and

I believe in me.

**NOVEMBER
26**

A lot

of things

in my life

are good.

NOVEMBER
27

It's okay
to ask for help
when I do
new things.

**NOVEMBER
28**

I can
give time to
family and friends
today.

NOVEMBER
29

I
have ways
to take care
of myself
and be safe.

NOVEMBER
30

I can
find solutions
by looking
inside of me.

DECEMBER
1

Today
I can tell
jokes with
my friends.

**DECEMBER
2**

I can
recognize
the things
I can change.

DECEMBER
3

I have
the right
to take the
time to do
the things I enjoy.

DECEMBER
4

I will
take time
to enjoy
each day.

**DECEMBER
5**

I believe
God looks
after me.

DECEMBER
6

There's

no one in

the world I'd

rather be than me.

DECEMBER
7

have many
feelings in
just one day.

DECEMBER
8

I
have fun
laughing
with my friends.

DECEMBER
9

Today
I will make
safe choices.

DECEMBER
10

With
help I can
learn to cope
with problems
in my family.

**DECEMBER
11**

Kids
come in all
sizes, shapes,
and COLORS --
every kid is special.

**DECEMBER
12**

can accept
things
I can't change.

**DECEMBER
13**

I have
the right
to get help.

I can
spend time
with my
friends today.

DECEMBER
15

Today
I celebrate
that God
loves me.

DECEMBER
16

Today is

a new

beginning.

DECEMBER
17

Today
I will pay
attention
to my feelings.

**DECEMBER
18**

I am
grateful
for
my friends.

DECEMBER
19

can find
places where
I am safe.

DECEMBER
20

I am
learning to
deal with
life's problems.

**DECEMBER
21**

I grow
more special
each and
every day.

DECEMBER
22

am learning
to make
healthy choices.

**DECEMBER
23**

I have
the right
to take good
care of myself.

**DECEMBER
24**

Today
I will
take care
of me.

DECEMBER
25

I believe
God cares
about me.

DECEMBER
26

Today I
will share my
special talents
with others.

DECEMBER
27

All
my feelings
are okay.

DECEMBER
28

There are
special people
in my life.
I am not alone.

DECEMBER
29

have many

new ways

to stay safe.

DECEMBER
30

As I end the
year today,
I'm a special kid.
Hooray!

**DECEMBER
31**

Appendix A
Resource List

Here are some phone numbers for you to call if you need help.

Boystown National Hotline 1-800-448-3000

Childhelp USA Child Abuse Hotline 1-800-422-4453

National Youth Crisis Hotline 1-800-448-4663

Remember that these calls won't cost you anything because they have a toll free area code of "800".

Appendix B
Introduction for Adults

Welcome to *Kids' Power, Too: Words to Grow By*. This is a book of daily affirmations written specifically for youngsters. Yet *Kids' Power, Too* also speaks to that precious and beautiful child in each and every one of us. Affirmations are positive statements detailing healthy ways people can act, feel, and think. They provide opportunities to develop new attitudes and skills in positively coping with life one day at a time.

Growing up in today's world can be a major challenge for all children. Families, schools, and communities are dealing with multiple stressors, including divorce, violence, abuse, alcoholism and other drug addiction, mental-health problems, death, crime and incarceration, illness, unemployment, and poverty. *Kids' Power, Too* is designed to help youngsters feel better about themselves and positively cope with the many challenges they face. The affirmations are aimed at assisting children to take better care of themselves, to stay safe, and move toward more balanced and healthy lives. These daily thoughts not only help youngsters see that they are special and valued people but also to acknowledge and further develop their own strengths. Research indicates that children develop strengths and resiliency if they have access to an adult who is caring and supportive, have opportunities for active participation, and are challenged with high expectations within their families, schools, and communities.

Affirmation Themes

Kids' Power, Too is based on five major messages that help children develop their strengths and resiliency:

I Am	*I am likeable, capable, unique, and valued.*
I Can	*I can achieve my goals.*
I Have	*I have strengths, capabilities, and people who will help me.*
I Will	*I will share my skills and knowledge with others.*
I Believe	*I believe in something greater than myself.* *

The affirmations represent ten themes: **Celebration, Feelings, Family and Friends, Safety, Challenges/Problem Solving, Being a Kid, Choices, Rights, Self-Care,** and **Spirituality**. These themes appear regularly throughout the book, and the affirmations build on one another.

* *We are gratefully indebted to Family Connection, a program of Rainbow Days, Inc., for permission to use these five major messages.*

Settings

Kids' Power, Too can be used effectively in a variety of settings:

● *Prevention/Intervention Programs*

Kids' Power, Too may be used in both community-and school-based programs, including student assistance and educational support groups. The facilitator or a designated child can read a daily affirmation at the beginning and/or close of each group.

- *Counseling/Therapy Programs*
The daily readings can be used in various counseling situations to empower individuals to cope more proactively with the problems and issues they face. Among the many possible settings are facilities for treating alcohol and other drug addiction, shelters for battered women and children, outpatient mental-health clinics, family or child guidance programs, and individual therapy.

- *Classrooms*
Teachers in elementary schools can share an affirmation with the class each day to remind children of their special qualities and assist them in developing skills to handle life's challenges in positive ways. Doing so can enhance children's self-esteem.

- *Religious Groups*
Kids' Power, Too can be integrated into youth groups to help youngsters develop a variety of healthy living skills. Many of the affirmations support children in developing and deepening their sense of spiritually.

- *Community Recreation Programs*
The affirmations can be used in a variety of community programs to reinforce efforts to help children value themselves, develop positive friendships, and grow up healthy.

- *At Home*
Parents, guardians, and other loving adults may want to use this book at home with their children.

Guidelines for Use

Children can read *Kids' Power, Too* independently or with the support of a loving parent or other caring adult. If you are this supportive person, here are some helpful guidelines to keep in mind:

• **Read through the book first** so you are familiar with the messages. That way, you can reinforce the positive thoughts and affirmations with the children in your life.

• **Allow children to use the book in their own way.** Let them guide this process. Allow them to be kids.

• **In discussing affirmations with children**, remember to listen to and validate their feelings, thoughts, perceptions, and responses.

• **Be respectful.** Ask childrens' permission before discussing their thoughts and feelings.

• **Keep in mind that some children may choose to use this book alone.** Simply introducing them to the book and being available for follow-up at their request may suffice.

• **You can read the affirmations to younger children** so they can benefit as well.

• **Encourage children to write, color, or draw in *Kids' Power, Too*.** Encourage them to jot down their thoughts, copy an affirmation in their own writing, and express themselves creatively. (It is important for children from the same family to each have their own copy.)

• **Help** each child find a safe place to keep his or her book.

- **Family rituals are important to children.** If a child wishes, schedule a special time each day for sharing the book. Put everything else aside at this time and give the youngster your undivided attention.

- **Occasionally affirmations may bring up powerful issues and feelings for a child.** Do not hesitate to get professional assistance from a therapist or counselor when needed.

Good luck on your journey. We hope this book supports your efforts in helping children build strengths and resiliency. We hope these affirmations help your youngsters grow into healthy, capable, and competent people. May children of all ages come to realize in their hearts that they are filled with beauty and worth. May they learn to accept, celebrate, and use their unique gifts not only for their own benefit, but for the benefit of others.

ImaginWorks

8300 Douglas
Suite 701
Dallas, Texas 75225

ORDER FORM

Ship to: _____

_____

_____

_____

Bill to: _____

_____

_____

_____

Qty	Title	$ Each	$ Amount
	Kids' Power, Too . . . Words to Grow By	$12.95	
Other important titles to read . . .			
	Kids' Power: Healing Games for Children of Alcoholics	$ 9.95	
	Conducting Support Groups for Elementary Children	$13.95	
	Discovery . . . Finding the Buried Treasure	$14.95	
	Amount of Order		
	Sales Tax (TX residents)		
	Shipping (10% of Amount of Order)		
Enclose Check or Money Order in US dollars as payment.	TOTAL		

Thank you for your order!